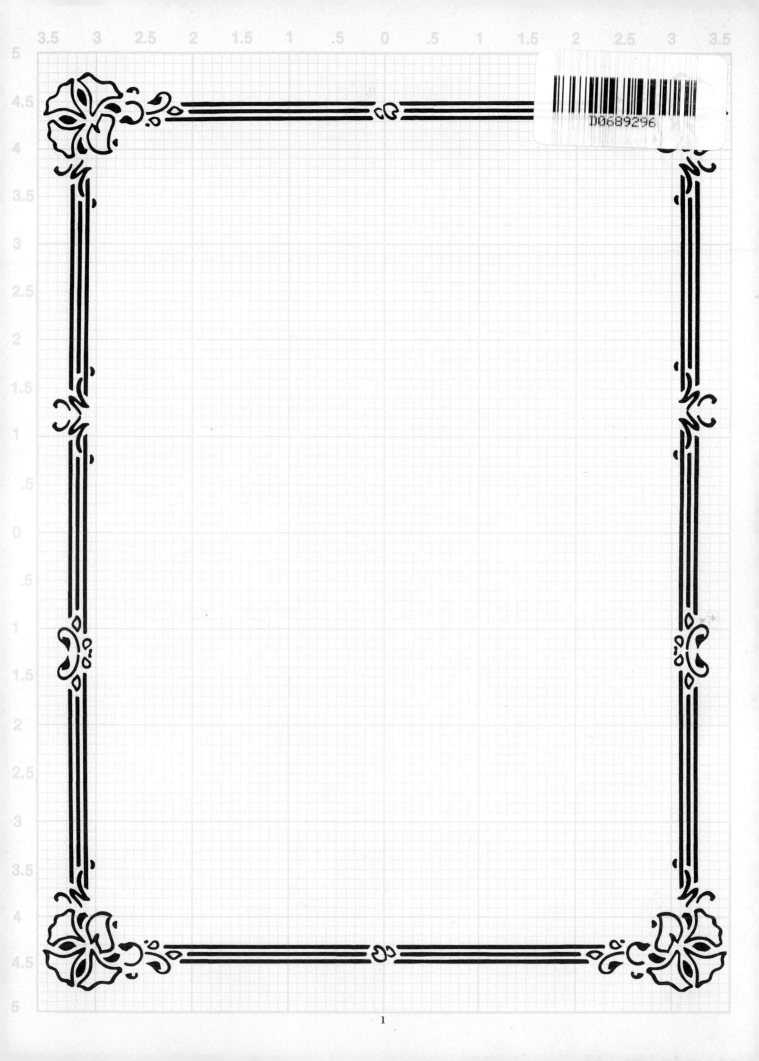

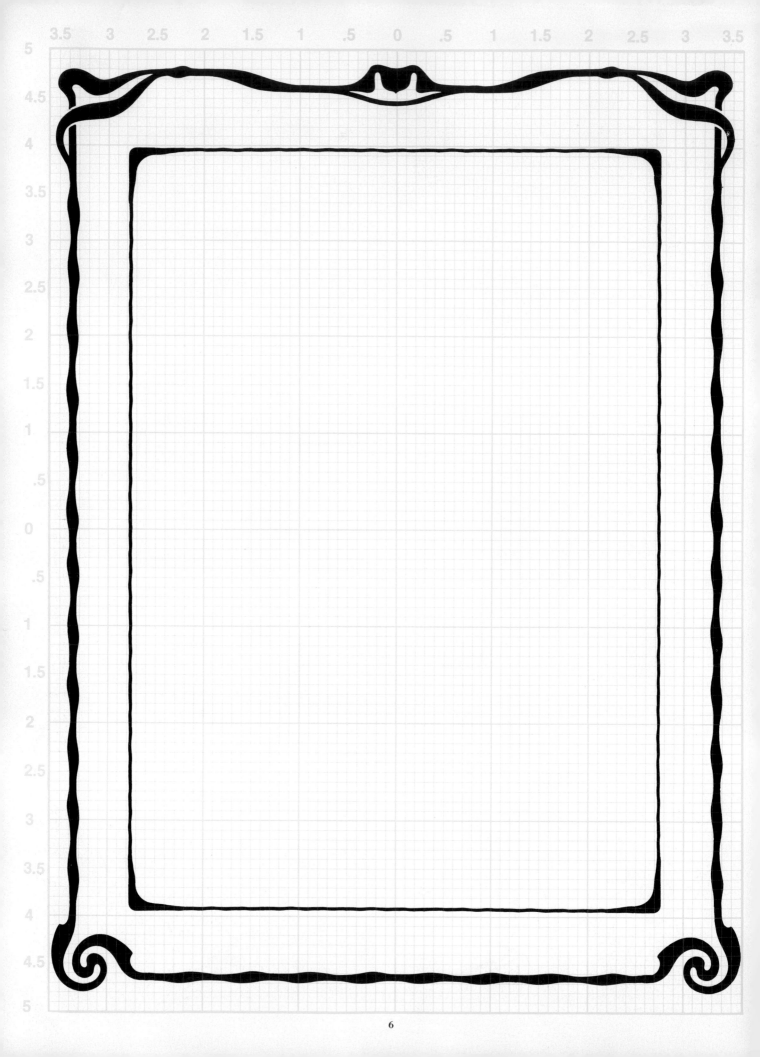

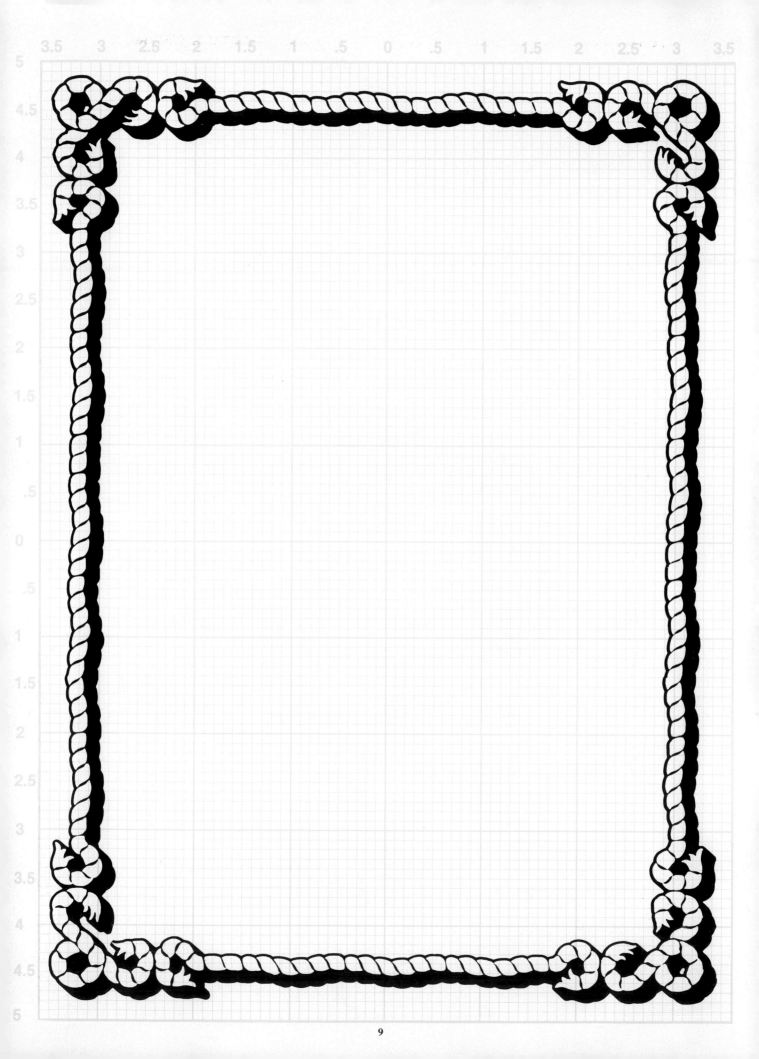

This book is dedicated
with love
to my parents,
Betty Heller Katzen and Leon Katzen;
and to their mothers,
Minnie Handleman Heller
(1892-1968)
and
Mollie Berman Katzen
(1883-1943).

# ✦ ACKNOWLEDGEMENTS ✦

It is a joy for me to acknowledge the people who have enabled me to begin, sustain, and complete this project:

Hal Hershey ~ friend, mentor, office-mate, and seasoned book-designer, whose balanced, honest feedback on every aspect of this book has helped to clear my vision, and whose detailed assistance has been indispensible to the production of this book; Jeffrey Black ~ whose love, patience, and enthusiasm fed me steadily during the final year of intense work on this project, and whose companionship has greatly lightened up my heart; Ezra K. Katzen ~ brother to me, and special counsel, literary agent, and godfather to this book; Buffalo ~ my step-dog, whose sunny presence kept me going on many foggy days; Meredith Barchat, Patricia Dustan, Sarah Gowin, Susan Ostertag, and Sarah Sutro ~ extraordinary friends, each of whom has had a special relationship with ~and influence upon— The Enchanted Broccoli Forest; Brenton Beck (of Fifth Street Design, Berkeley) ~ whose graphic work has inspired me, and who has given me invaluable assistance in the production of the cover; Jane Rockwell ~ who took time away from her own

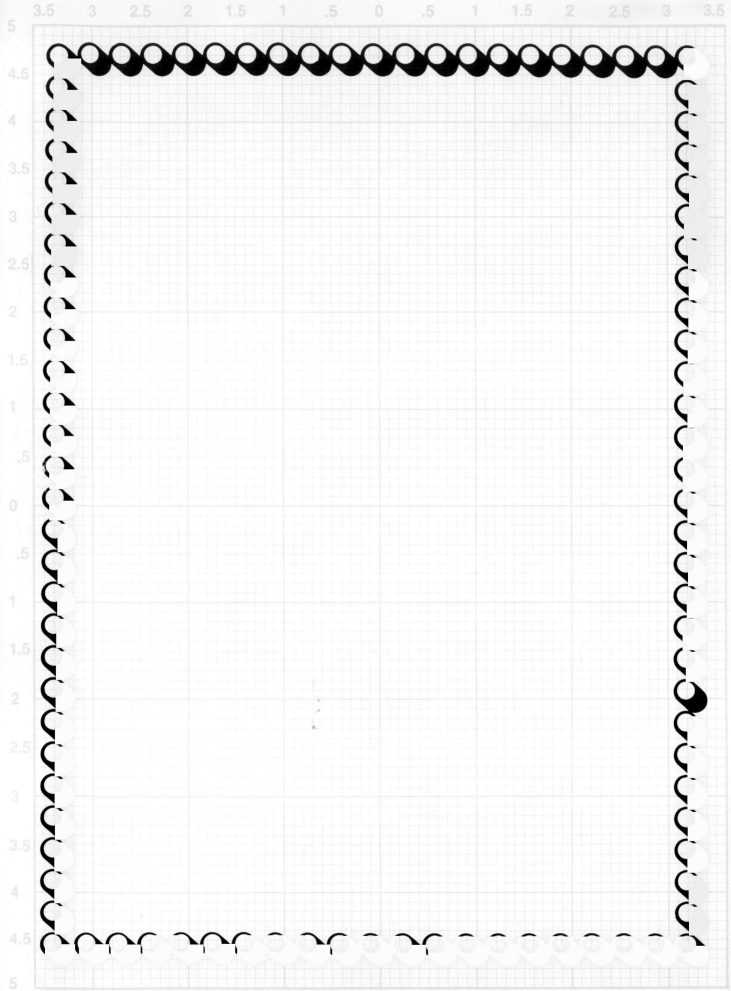

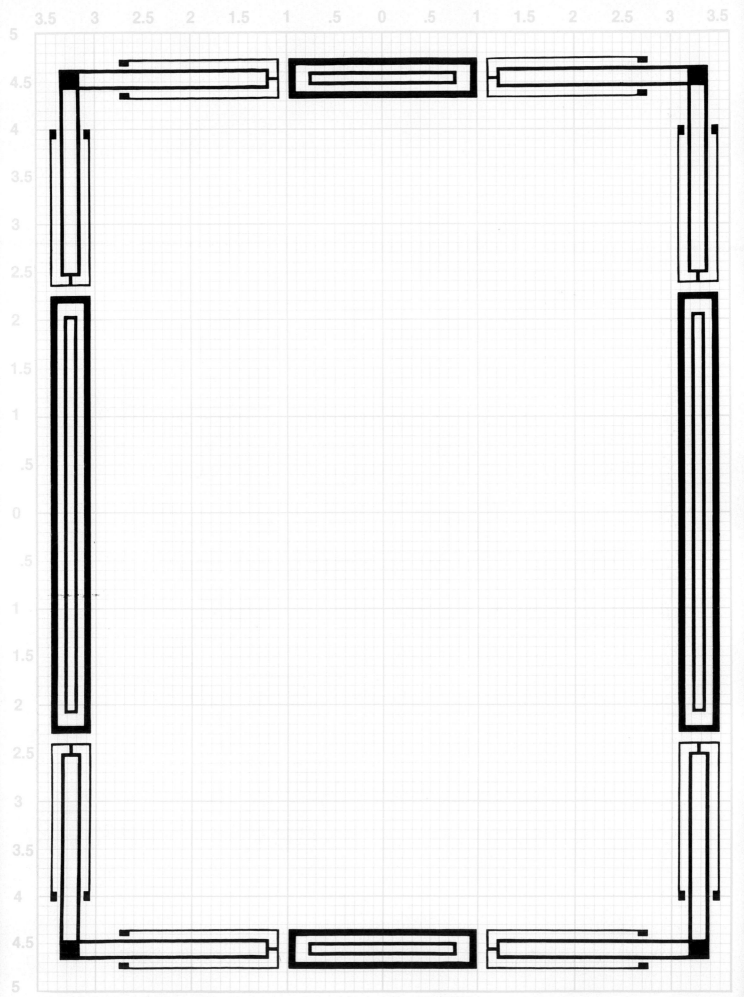

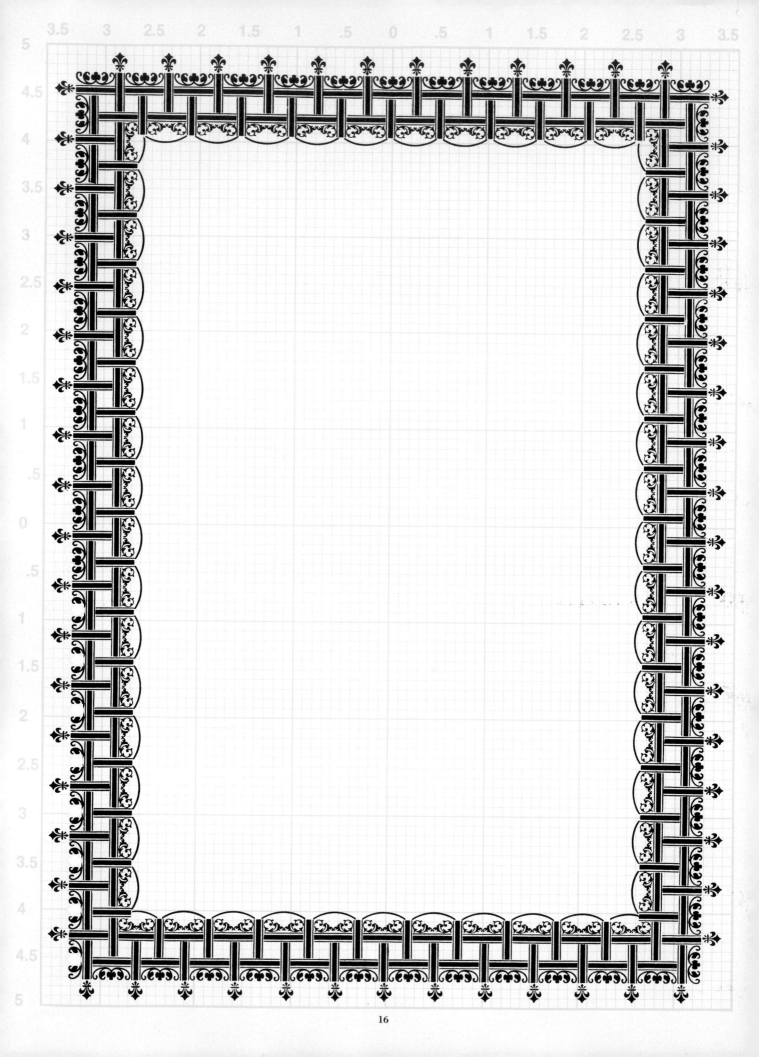

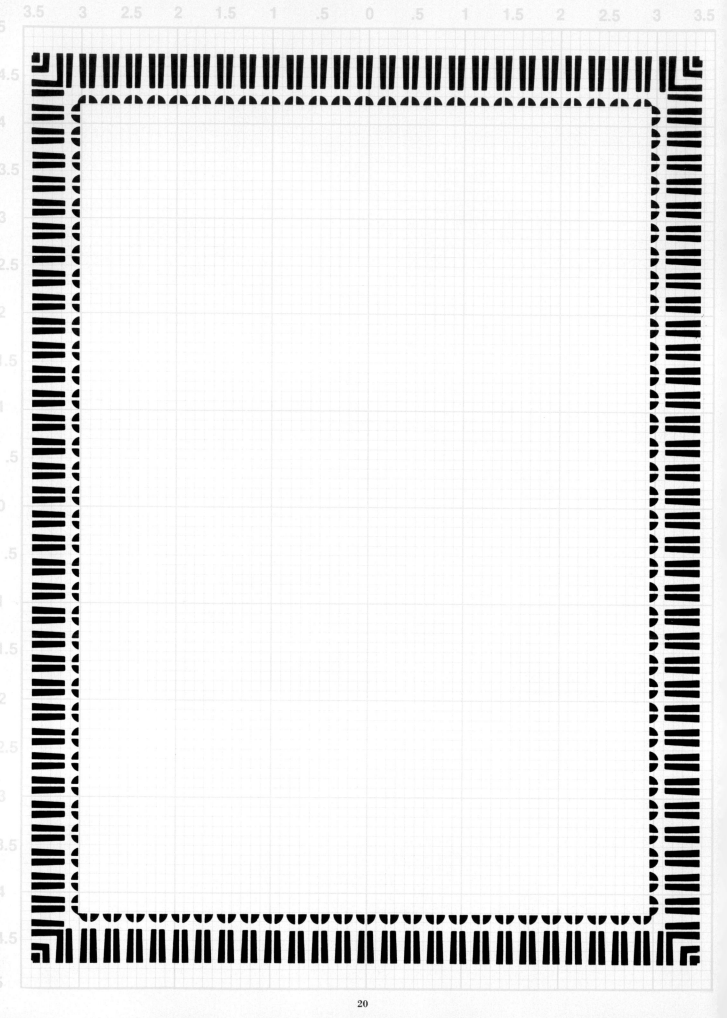

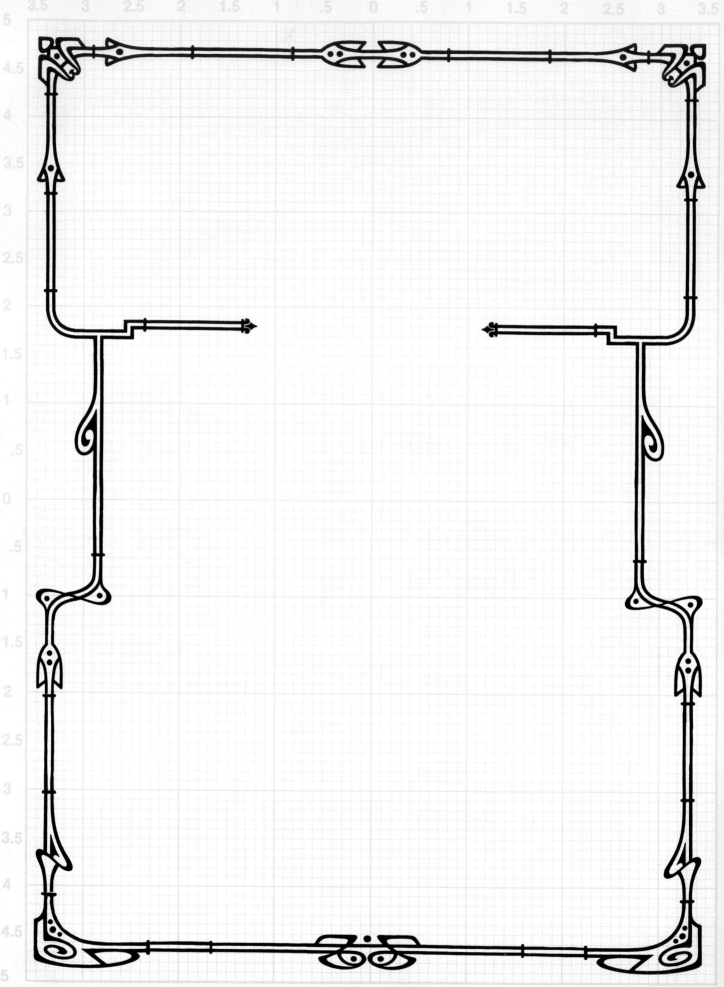

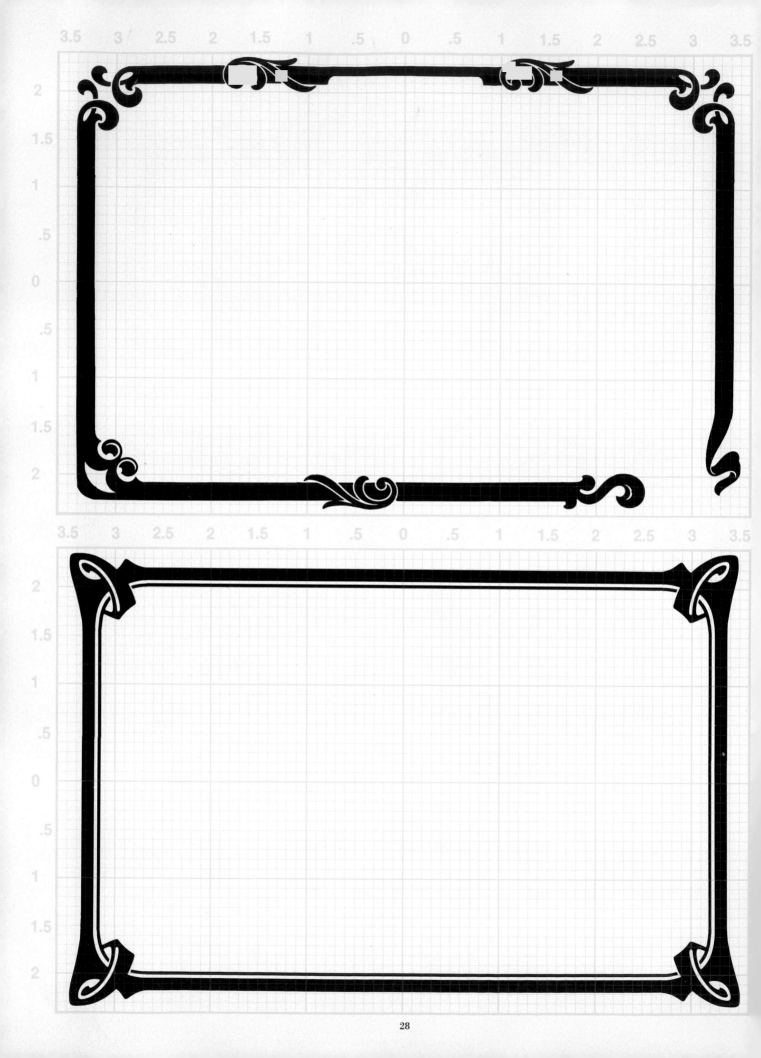

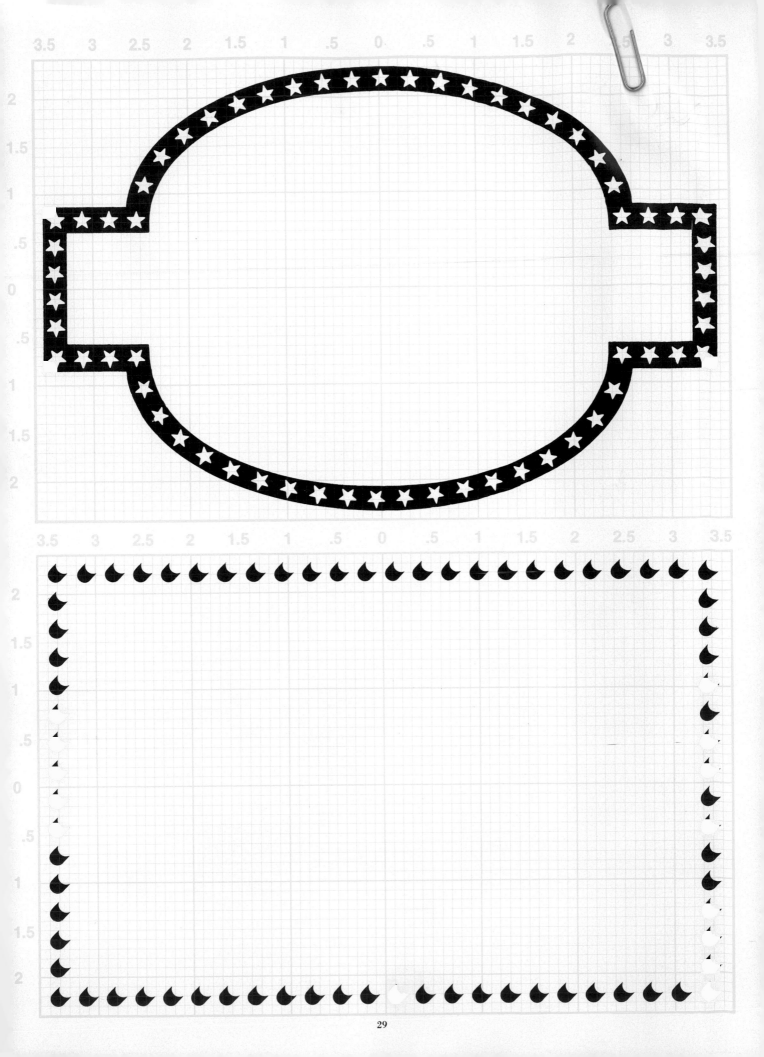